Rookie
reader

SHOW-AND-TELL
SAM

BY
CHARNAN
SIMON

ILLUSTRATED
BY
GARY BIALKE

CHILDREN'S PRESS ®
A Division of Grolier Publishing
New York • London • Hong Kong • Sydney
Danbury, Connecticut

For Millie, Maude, and Riley,
who all know how to behave in school.
—C. S.

For Ms. Shlobotnik, who always said I'd excel in "Nap Time
—G. B.

Reading Consultant
Linda Cornwell
Learning Resource Consultant
Indiana Department of Education

Visit Children's Press® on the Internet at:
http://publishing.grolier.com

Library of Congress Cataloging-in-Publication Data

Simon, Charnan.
    Show-and-tell Sam / by Charnan Simon ; illustrated by Gary Bialke.
        p. cm. — (A rookie reader)
    Summary: Rosie brings her dog Sam to school for show-and-tell.
    ISBN 0-516-20945-0 (lib.bdg.)   0-516-26413-3 (pbk.)
    [1. Dogs—Fiction. 2. Schools—Fiction.] I. Bialke, Gary, ill. II. Title. III. Series.
PZ7.S6035Sh   1998
[E] —dc21   97-40044
                                                                CIP
                                                                 AC

Rosie's dog Sam
was going to school.

3

"You can be my show-and-tell,"
Rosie said.

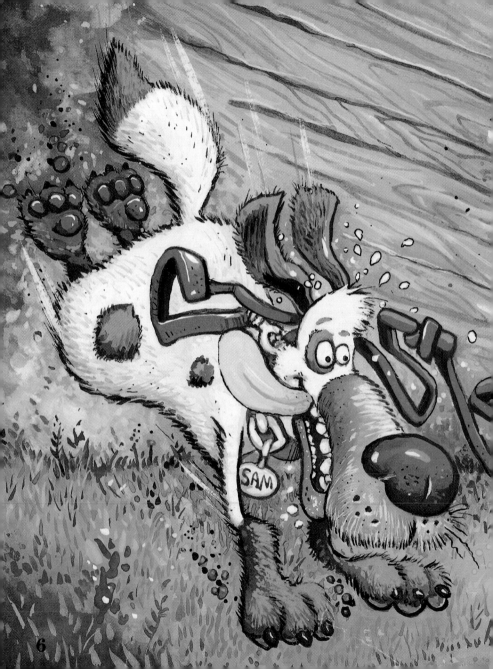

Sam could hardly wait.

He showed Rosie
a shortcut to school,

9

and how to line up at the door.

10

Sam showed Rosie's class
a new way to paint,

13

and sharpen pencils.

15

He showed them how
much he liked Teacher,

and tadpoles,

18

and best of all—snack time!

Sam could tell
the class liked him, too.

Rosie's dog Sam
still goes to school.

He misses snack time.

ABOUT THE AUTHOR

Charnan Simon has been an editor for *Cricket* magazine and sometimes works at a children's bookstore called Pooh Corner. Mainly, though, she spends her time reading and writing books. Charnan lives in Madison, Wisconsin, with her husband Tom Kazunas, her daughters Ariel and Hana, and the real Sam. This Sam is part collie and part golden retriever, and he loved going to puppy kindergarten, even if he was never promoted to first grade. Other Rookie Readers about Sam include *Sam the Garbage Hound, Sam and Dasher,* and *Guard the House, Sam!*

ABOUT THE ILLUSTRATOR

Gary Bialke lives in the upper left-hand corner of the United States with five shedding machines. This is not "normal." He barks at strangers and sleeps twenty hours a day. It's only his long hind legs and opposable thumbs that make him the pack leader. He is loved by veterinarians everywhere.